Contents

Preface

Beginning Bass Guitar is a presumptuous title. After all, how can this small volume tell you everything there is to know about playing bass? Well, it can't. There are many things about playing any instrument that simply cannot be conveyed at all on the printed page. But be not discouraged. Crammed between these covers is enough basic instruction and valuable information not only to get you started on the right foot, but to keep you busy for a good long while. If you really use this book well, you will learn the hows and whys of simple root/fifth lines all the way through advanced techniques and styles.

The manner in which this book is set up has a lot to do with the way that I think people learn best. You may have seen, or even used, methods that try to explain everything theoretically before letting you play anything. Or perhaps you have had experience with instruction books that deal with simple concepts so long-windedly that you are never quite sure where you stand ("When you have mastered the playing of these three notes, in order, proceed to practice this sequence in every key, at slow, medium, and fast tempos…"). What I have tried to do here is to give you concepts and techniques that will help you to form a firm foundation for your own development and musical growth. Every item of information has been included for a reason and there is no excess filler.

Whether you are a total beginner, or have already been playing for a while, I would hope that you will go straight through this book from beginning to end. The very nature of learning to play an instrument, and of music in general, makes it necessary to introduce certain ideas at certain times. The limitations of space and the printed page have also affected the presentation of the material. Add to this the fact that you are only one of thousands who will use this book, each of you with your own proclivities, strengths, weaknesses, and learning pace, and you will understand why, at times, you may feel that we are dwelling too long on one point or glossing over another where you would welcome a fuller explanation. In short, to get the most out of this book, you've got to trust me.

To sum it up, the object of **Beginning Bass Guitar** is not to tell you everything there is to know about playing bass. I don't think that I would do that even if I could - it would take all the fun out of it for you. I am sure that when you have gone through this book thoroughly, and understand all that has been said, you will still have questions. However, I am equally confident that your working knowledge of music and bass playing will enable you to find the answers in other books, from other players, or just by keeping your eyes and ears open when listening to live or recorded music. In short, if you study well and practice regularly, this book will guide you through the morass of beginnerdom and up into the rarefied atmosphere of the competent musician.

The Basics

For those of you who are just starting out, these beginning instructions are a must. Even if you have been playing bass for a while, take some time to go over what is said here. When we get into more advanced techniques later on, it will be important to understand the basics as set forth in this chapter.

Holding the Bass

You will probably do most of your practicing sitting down. Place the bass on your right thigh. Hold it against your body and let your right forearm rest comfortably on top. Your right elbow should be fairly close to your body.

One thing you will soon notice about playing bass in a sitting position is that it is easy to tense up if you are not careful. This can really hurt your playing—if your body is tense, your music will sound tense. Especially while practicing, it is important to make a conscious effort to remain relaxed. Changing your position slightly from time to time can help: Cross your legs, lean back a little in your chair, sit on the edge of your chair with ankles crossed; small variations in position such as these will keep muscle tension away.

For playing in a standing position you will need a strap. If you don't already have a strap you can get one at any music store for about three or four dollars. (Most straps are not labeled specifically as "bass straps" but rather as simply "guitar straps." These are okay.)

Many players adjust their straps so that the bass hangs at waist level or even lower. They do this for looks only. This kind of low-slung position limits the mobility of both left and right hands and will make accurate playing much more difficult. I won't say that appearance is not important and eventually you may want to (or have to) go with this look. However, as you are starting out you may as well make things as easy on yourself as you can.

To adjust the strap, attach it to the bass and place it over your left shoulder. While sitting and holding the bass in your usual playing position, adjust the strap until it is just taut. Now, when you stand up the strap will hold the bass in the same position, relative to your body, as it is when you are sitting.

Tuning

Here are four ways to get in tune.

RELATIVE TUNING

If you know that your bass is close to pitch you can use this method to make sure that it is in tune with itself:

- Fret the E, or fourth, string at the fifth fret. This note is A and should sound the same as the open A, or third, string. If the A string does not sound in tune, loosen it until it sounds lower than the fourth string, fifth fret. Slowly bring it up to pitch.

- When your A string is in tune, fret it at the fifth fret. This note is D and should sound the same as the open D, or second, string.

- When your D string is in tune, fret it at the fifth fret. This note is G and should sound the same as the open G, or first, string.

This diagram summarizes the relative tuning method:

When you understand this relationship, you can use it to check any string against another. So if someone gives just one note, for instance an A, and you get one string in tune, you can tune the other three from there.

TUNING BY HARMONICS

Harmonics are tones produced without actually fretting a string. Instead, just touch the string lightly with a left-hand finger directly above the fret indicated. Strike (pluck) the string with your right-hand index or middle finger and remove the left-hand finger immediately. The result is a high, bell-like tone. In fact, harmonics are often referred to as 'chimes'. The easiest harmonics to sound are those produced by touching the strings at the twelfth fret. Try a few of these to get the idea before proceeding.

Like the relative tuning method above, this method can only tell you if your bass is in tune to itself. If you are playing with other people you will need to tune at least one of your strings to them before applying this method.

- Assuming that your E (fourth) string is in tune, sound the harmonic at the fifth fret. This tone (E) should sound the same as the harmonic on the A (third) string, seventh fret. If the two tones are not perfectly in unison, loosen the A string until it sounds lower and then slowly bring it up to pitch.*

---

* You can see that an advantage of this method over the relative tuning method is that both tones keep ringing while you are tuning, making comparison easier.

Miles Davis and Marcus Miller

- When your A string is in tune, sound its harmonic at the fifth fret. Compare and match this tone (A) to the harmonic on the D (second) string, seventh fret.

- When your D string is in tune, sound its harmonic at the fifth fret. Compare and match this tone (D) to the harmonic on the G (first) string, seventh fret.

This diagram summarizes tuning by harmonics:

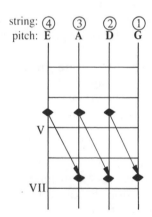

TUNING TO A GUITAR

Since the four bass strings are tuned to the same pitches as the four lowest guitar strings but one octave lower, it is a pretty simple matter to get in tune with a guitarist.

To make it easier to compare and match the pitch of each string, sound each of your strings as a harmonic at the twelfth fret. When you do this, your strings will sound exactly the same pitches as those of the guitar:

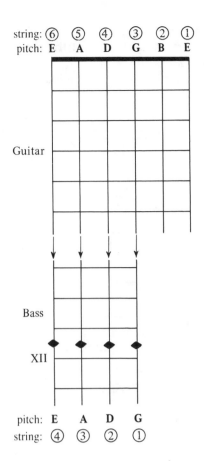

TUNING TO A PIANO OR OTHER KEYBOARD INSTRUMENT

Here are the notes that correspond to the open strings of the bass:*

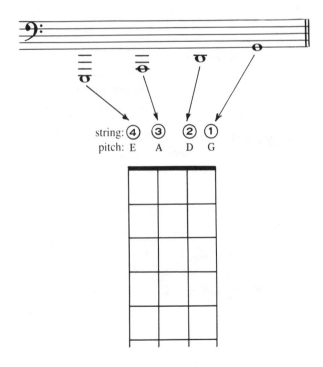

---

* These notes represent the actual sounds of the bass strings. Music for bass is written one octave higher than it sounds to make it easier to read.

It may be easier for you to hear these tones accurately if you sound them as harmonics at the twelfth fret. This makes them sound one octave higher. Harmonics also have a purer tone, making the actual pitch more distinguishable.

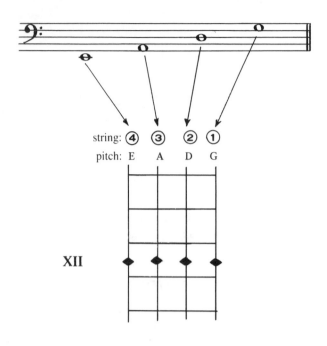

Left- and Right-Hand Technique

When you play bass you bring both hands into contact with the strings. That may sound a bit obvious but it is a fact that is true of very few stringed instruments. A violinist uses a bow, many guitarists play with picks, and keyboard players are separated from their strings by complex mechanical actions. The bass player, except when playing an open string, must touch the string with both hands to produce each note. Because of this, there are many left- and right-hand techniques we can use to affect the attack, tone, and duration of each note. We will explore a lot of advanced techniques—damping, thumb slaps, hammerons, **et al.**—before we are through. Right now we will focus on the best way to produce a clear, clean sound.

LEFT HAND

In order to fret a string, your left-hand fingertip must press it to the fingerboard just behind (to the left of) the fret. There are several things to keep in mind that will help you get a clear sound on fretted notes:

- **Use the fingertips**. Arch your fingers so that they come straight down on the strings. Think of making an "OK" sign with your thumb and forefinger.

- **Keep your thumb in the middle of the back of the neck**. Although it is tempting to let your thumb slide up and peek over the top of the neck, keeping it in the middle, approximately opposite the middle finger, will help your fingers to stay properly arched.

- **Keep your wrist low and your elbow close to the body**. This will also help you to bring your fingers down accurately and with the most power possible.

- **Avoid tensing your shoulder**. This can creep up on you and severely limit your mobility. If your shoulder and arm are not relaxed it can be difficult to change positions (move up and down the neck) smoothly.

RIGHT HAND

There are two major approaches to right-hand technique: fingerstyle and playing with a pick. Throughout most of this book we will be dealing with fingerstyle because it is the more versatile of the two techniques.*

Most bass players use primarily the index and middle fingers when playing fingerstyle. The thumb and ring finger are used to a lesser degree. (The little finger is not used at all.) Try playing the G (first) string with first your index finger and then your middle finger. Alternate the two fingers slowly and evenly while you read the following:

- **Use rest strokes**. A **rest stroke** is when your finger moves straight across the string to be played and comes to rest on the next lower string. The positive feel you get by using rest strokes ensures evenness of attack and tone and also helps your rhythm and timekeeping.

- **Keep your fingers straight**. With each stroke your finger should move from the knuckle.

- **Arch your wrist**. This helps you to keep your fingers straight.

- **Make sure that your fingers move straight across the strings**. In other words, the fingers should be perpendicular to the strings. Extending your thumb a bit to the left will help pull your hand into line.

---

* For information on playing with a pick, see "Rock" and "New Wave" sections of the "Styles" chapter.

Reading Music and Tablature

The subject of reading music can be a sore point for many musicians. Many self-taught players, or those who play "by ear," actively scorn the idea of learning a song from the printed page. (**Rock Bass Player:** "Hey man, do you know how to read music?" **Country Bass Player:** "Not enough to hurt my playin'.")

With all styles of music becoming more complex, this attitude is fading. Musicians from country to new wave are realizing that it is not only the studio hotshots who need to be musically literate. Reading music, even if it is only interpreting a set of chord changes hastily scribbled on a Burger King napkin, saves time in rehearsal, facilitates communication among band members, makes it easier to learn and remember tunes, and makes you a more well-rounded musician in general.

Aside from all of that, if you are to get anything from this book, we will need a means of communicating. The system of notation used in this book will make the process of understanding written music as painless as possible. The use of **tablature**, a graphic representation of the bass neck, will ease you into the concept of interpreting music from the printed page with the result that you should come out of this book with a fair amount of reading skill.

STANDARD NOTATION

If you already know something about reading music, this section will show you how standard music notation relates specifically to the bass. If you are a total stranger to written music, you will find out what you need to know to start right in playing the music in this book.

Notes in the Bass Clef

Music for any instrument is written by placing notes on a **staff** of five lines (and four spaces). Music for bass is written in the **bass clef.** The bass clef symbol appears at the beginning of each staff.

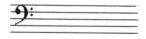

Here are notes positioned on the staff to represent the open strings of the bass:

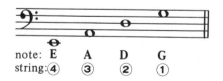

You can see that the range of the bass fits comfortably in and around the staff. Notes that go above or below the staff, such as the open E string, are written on temporary extensions of the staff called **leger lines.**

Here is a chart of all the notes in the area covered by the first five frets, commonly known as **first position:**

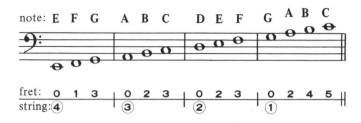

The notes in the example above are called **natural** notes. Any one of these natural notes may be affected by a **sharp** or a **flat.** A sharp (♯) in front of a note raises that note one half-step, which is equal to one fret on the bass. A flat (♭) lowers the note that follows it by one half-step.* Since some of the natural notes are only one fret apart to begin with, they are not often altered by sharps or flats. For example, B is played on the third string, second fret; C is played on the third string, third fret. Since a sharp raises a note by one fret, B-sharp would sound the same as C-natural. By the same token C-flat would sound the same as B-natural. Notes that sound the same but that are written differently are said to be **enharmonic.**

Here are the notes in first position going up by half steps written out using sharps. (Enharmonic equivalents are shown in parentheses.)

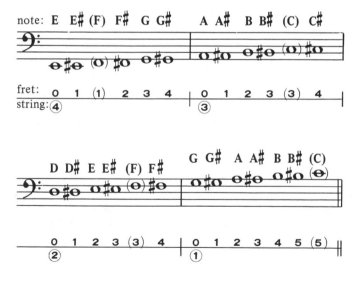

---

* When sharps and flats occur in the middle of a piece of music, they are called **accidentals.** Accidentals affect only the note to which they are applied, and any other note of the same pitch, for the duration of the measure.

Now we'll come back down through all the same notes notating them with flats.

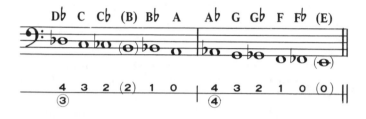

Comparing these last two examples you will find a lot of enharmonic equivalents. For example, fourth string, second fret can be written as either F-sharp or G-flat.

All of this may seem to be a lot to take in all at once, but don't worry about getting it all down cold right away. The best way to absorb this kind of information is to just get used to it. In a very short while we will get into playing some actual bass-lines and, little by little, reading music and tablature will become second nature to you.

TABLATURE

Tablature is a system of notation that in many ways resembles standard music notation but is tailored to a specific stringed instrument—in this case, bass. Tablature has a long and venerable history dating back to lute music of the Renaissance but here is an explanation of the modern system used in this book.

Like the staff used in standard notation, the tablature staff has five lines. However, in tablature only the four spaces in between the lines are used. Each space represents a string of the bass.

Numbers placed in each space denote frets along the particular string. (A zero denotes an open string.)

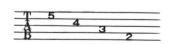

RHYTHM

With tablature to show you where to put your fingers, you now need to know how long to hold each note. With few exceptions rhythm is expressed the same way in both standard notation and tablature.

First let's look at the different types of notes, each of which stands for a different duration of sound.

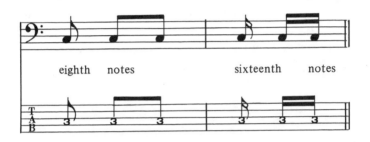

Although the relative duration of these types of notes one to another remains the same no matter at what speed you are playing, the way in which they relate to the **beat** or **meter** is fixed by the **time signature** found at the beginning of the music. It is the time signature that tells you how many beats there are per **measure** (or **bar**) and what kind of note constitutes one beat. The most common time signature is $\frac{4}{4}$. In fact it is often referred to as **common time** and abbreviated as **C**.

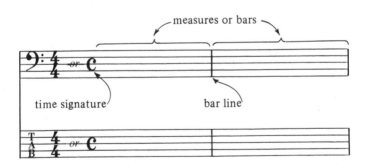

The top **4** of $\frac{4}{4}$ tells you that there are four beats in each measure. The bottom **4** means that a quarter note gets one beat. Try playing a few bars of $\frac{4}{4}$ time with four quarter-notes per measure. You can use a metronome or just tap your foot to keep the beat even. Here are four bars to start you off: Follow the count and give each quarter note the same time value.

In addition, each type of note has its corresponding **rest**. These stand for the corresponding time value of silence. This is what each kind of rest looks like:

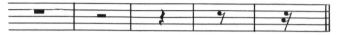

whole rest   half rest   quarter rest   eighth rest sixteenth rest

Things could get pretty dull if we played only four quarter-notes in every measure of $\frac{4}{4}$ time. If you think back to your grade school studies in fractions, I think that you will realize just how many different combinations can make up four quarters:

- one whole-note per measure

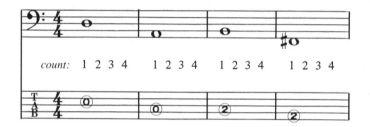

- two half-notes per measure

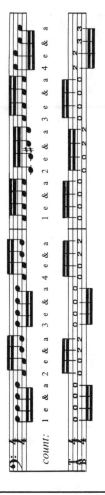

- eight eighth-notes

- sixteen sixteenth-notes

- or any combination of notes adding up to four quarters.

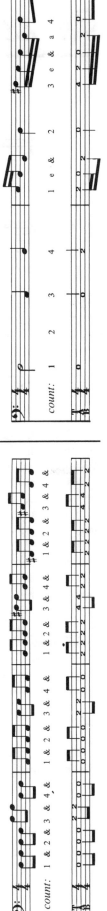

The Root / Fifth Relationship

If you play through the bass line above you may find it rather simplistic—almost idiotic—but, believe it or not, this type of pattern is what is often expected of the bass player: no more, no less. In addition, any time you hear the bass playing a more intricate bass part, you can be sure that the player is thinking of this type of simple line at some level as a point of departure.

As a bass player you are the "bottom" of the band. To be a good bass player (especially in rock and in country music) you must support the rest of the band by playing the most essential and basic notes of each chord. Temptation to the contrary, you must leave the more complex harmonic and melodic embellishment to guitar and keyboard players. The reward comes in knowing, and knowing that they know, that their flights of fancy would sound pretty shallow (if not downright silly) if you were not taking care of business holding down the low end.

With that in mind, let's explore just what is meant by the "essential and basic" notes of any chord.

Major Scales

Chords are formed by taking specific notes out of a **scale**. That is a pretty simplified explanation but it is enough for now as we start to look at some major scales.

For our first scale let's try C major. It is made up entirely of natural notes (no sharps or flats) and so should be easy to read. (The small numbers next to each note tell you which left-hand finger to use: **1** = index, **2** = middle, **3** = ring, **4** = pinky.)

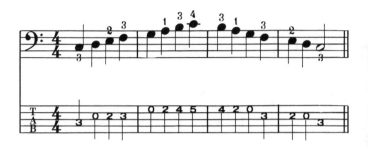

Sound familiar? The C major scale you have just played is in first position (first finger, first fret; second finger, second fret; etc.) except for the top three notes, which move you up to **second position** (first finger, second fret; second finger, third fret; etc.).

Here is the same C major scale played entirely in second position with no open strings:

The idea of playing things in positions is very important and I'll tell you why: If you can play something in one position without using open strings, you can move it anywhere on the neck and play it in any key. Let's take the second-position C scale and slide it up two frets to fourth position. Now you will be starting on the note D and so you will be playing a D major scale.

You can see that the relationship of the pitches to one another will remain the same no matter what fret you start on. Take some time to try this scale pattern all up and down the fretboard.

Taking this idea of moveable positions one step further, play the G major scale below.

It feels a lot like the C and D scales under your fingers. The fingering remains the same—only the strings have been changed. If we move our second-position G scale up to fourth position it becomes an A major scale:

As with the C scale, you can move this G scale up the neck until you run out of frets and it will still be the major scale of the note on which you start.

---

* Sharps or flats appearing at the beginning of each line of music constitute a **key signature**. In this case the key signature tells you that all Fs are played as F-sharps and that all Cs are played as C-sharps.

20

Roots and Fifths

The most important parts of any chord to a bass player are its **root** and its **fifth**. Since chords are made from notes selected from scales, you can probably guess what a fifth is: the fifth note of the scale. If you look back at the scales you have just played you can see that for the C scale, and so for a C chord as well, the root is C and the fifth is G:

Continuing up the scale you will find another C on top:

Extending the scale downward from the root discloses another fifth:

Just like the scale pattern, this pattern of roots and fifths may be moved anywhere on the neck.

It also follows that the pattern may be moved over a string to produce the root and fifth of a G scale or chord:

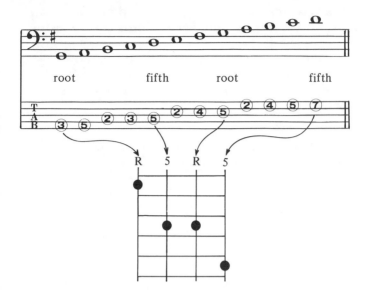

Jaco Pastorius

These two positions are the most important anchors that a bass player has. Try these simple bass lines to really get a feel for these essential positions.

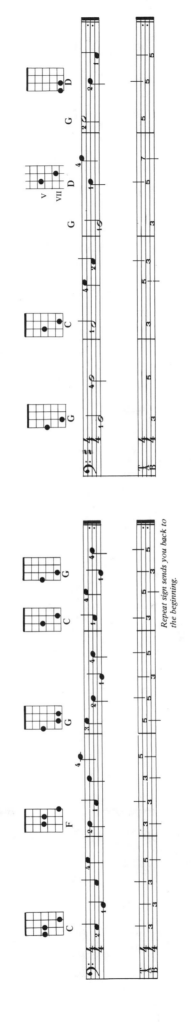

Repeat sign sends you back to the beginning.

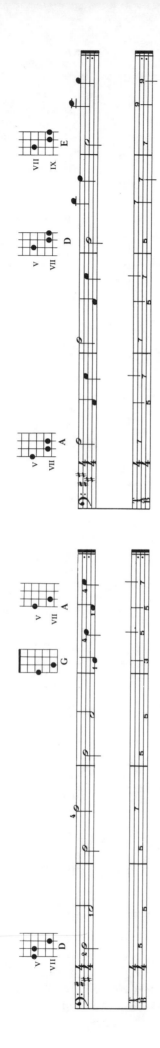

Before we start livening up these bass lines a bit, let's look at a few more handy fretboard patterns.

Naming Chords by Number

The chord progressions above are about as simple as they come. Although each progression uses different chords, the effect is quite similar. This is because within each progression, the three chords bear the same relationship to each other but each group of three belongs to a different key. Because these relationships are so standard, musicians often refer to chords within a key by number. Each set of three chords in the examples above consists of the I (one), IV (four), and V (five) chords of each key.

Key	I	IV	V
C	C	F	G
G	G	C	D
D	D	G	A
A	A	D	E

You can tell from the regular sound of these progressions how important it can be to know the position of the I, IV, and V chords in any key you happen to be playing in. Here are the fretboard patterns for the I, IV, and V chords when the root of the I chord is on the third (and first) string:

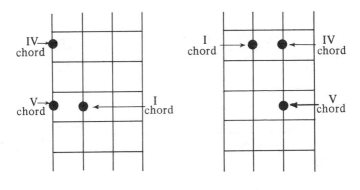

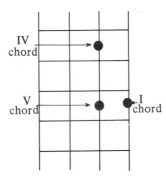

Move these over a string and you have the pattern of the roots of I, IV, and V chords when the root of the I chord is on the fourth (and second) string:

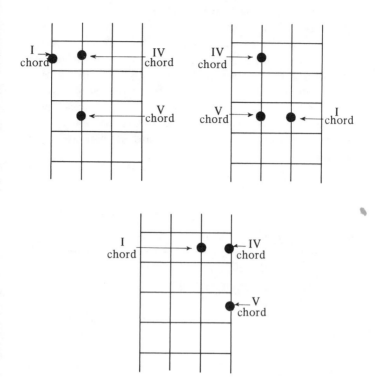

Here is the first of the sample bass-lines from the last section transposed from C up to E-flat. After you have recognized the patterns and how they work, try transposing this example to other keys.

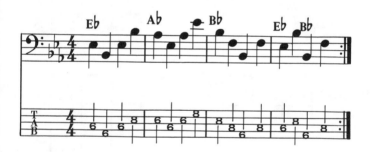

Now let's take the second of the examples and transpose it from G up to B:

Again, try moving this example around some more to really get the feel for the patterns of I, IV, and V chords.

26

Fills

In most styles of popular music the bass and drums play a fairly standardized rhythmic pattern throughout most of the song. Every two or four bars, however, one or both of them will usually vary the pattern a bit to "fill in" or punctuate the overall flow of the tune. These little figures are called **fills**. A fill can either be a simple device to keep rhythm and harmony moving or a dramatic punctuation between phrases or sections of a tune.

Walkups

The simplest fills are **scale runs**, short melodic fragments made up of notes from the major scale. A good example of this type of fill is a **walkup**:

A walkup may be found at the beginning of a tune or, very often, after a **stop** in the middle of a song. It is also a common device for announcing the beginning of a new verse or chorus. Here is a typical root/fifth bass-line with a sort of simple, country flavor that uses walkups at the beginning and in the middle. Play it at a moderate tempo and be careful not to rush the fills.

A walkup does not necessarily have to "walk up." Here are a few examples that "walk down"; that is, they approach the root of the following chord from above.

Paul McCartney

Chromatic Fills

Fills are not limited to scale tones. Since the roots of the IV and the V chords are both scale steps, this is a prime situation in which to introduce some **chromatic** ideas. (Whenever you hear the word 'chromatic', it refers to the concept of including notes from outside the scale.)

Here are a few typical bass parts in different styles incorporating simple fills.

Country

Watch out for the dotted quarter note in the next-to-last measure.

The symbol ♮ is a **natural sign**. It is an accidental the same as a sharp
(♯) or flat (♭). It is used in front of a note that has been sharped or
flatted by a previous accidental or by the key signature. Like an accidental sharp or flat, the natural affects only the pitch to which it is
applied (it has no effect on the same note in other octaves) and lasts
only for the duration of the measure in which it appears.

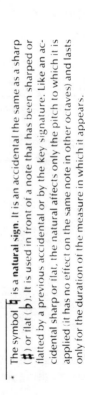

Soul

This James Brown-inspired bass-line is in $\frac{2}{4}$ time so there are only two quarter-note beats per measure. To get the rhythm in the last two bars it may help to think of the figure as.

Pop

This one is the kind of line you might find in a medium-tempo James Taylor tune.

Rock Ballad

Here is another time signature: $\frac{6}{4}$. It is used for slower rock tunes and some blues. Although $\frac{6}{4}$ literally means, "six beats per measure, quarter note gets one beat," it is most often felt, or counted, 'in two'. So if there were a measure of six quarter-notes, you would feel them as two groups of three with accents on **one** and **four** (>=accent):

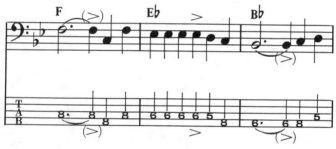

Putting a heavier accent on **four** produces a **backbeat**. Since it is common practice for the bass not to play on **four**, but to fill in on **five** and **six** and provide the secondary accent on **one**, the accents in parentheses will help you understand the feel in this example.

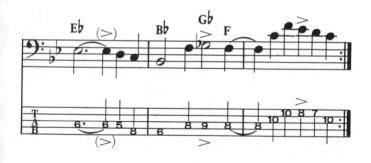

Right- and Left-Hand Damping

When practicing or playing you should always strive to give every note its full value. What this means is that you hold on to each note until you play the next one. When you are practicing alone this may sound a bit strange at first. When playing with a band, however, the bass player who leaves gaps between notes is punching holes in the music. There are special situations where cutting notes short (known as **staccato**) can be used to create an effect, but it is just that, a special effect.

Damping is a technique that is used to stop a note from ringing. You can damp an open string with either hand by just touching it enough to stop it vibrating. To damp a fretted string just release the pressure of the left-hand finger fretting the note but don't lift the finger completely off the string until it has stopped ringing. Bringing a right-hand finger in contact with a string, either in preparation for a rest stroke on that string or as the completion of a rest stroke on the next higher string, will also effectively damp the ringing string.

If you play the following pattern with rest strokes, you will find that cutting off each note is taken care of by the execution of the next.

In this type of situation you must be sure that you give each note its full duration. If you release pressure with the left-hand fretting finger, or bring a right-hand finger into contact with the string, it will stop the note prematurely.

In this next example you have just the opposite problem:

With each subsequent note on a lower or nonadjacent string you must use left-hand damping to stop each note just as you play the next.

Will Lee

Now here are some bass lines which include some staccato playing. Whenever you see a dot above or below the notehead or number, cut that note short. Staccato is most often used to point up **syncopation** (irregular rhythm or displaced accents).

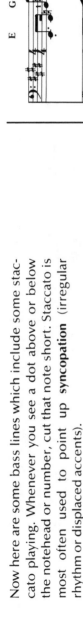

In the second example you have to damp the open E string. You can do this with either the left hand, right hand, or both.

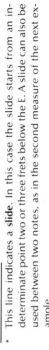

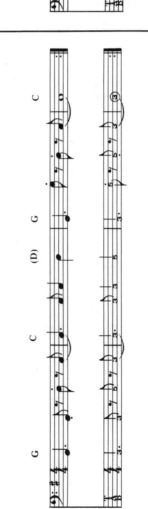

* This line indicates a **slide**. In this case the slide starts from an indeterminate point two or three frets below the E. A slide can also be used between two notes, as in the second measure of the next example.

Chords

Although we never (that is, seldom) play full chords on bass, it is very important to know how chords are constructed. Since you already know how to find the fifth of the chord given the root, let's look at what is missing.

Major and Minor Chords

Here are the patterns for an A major chord and an A minor chord.

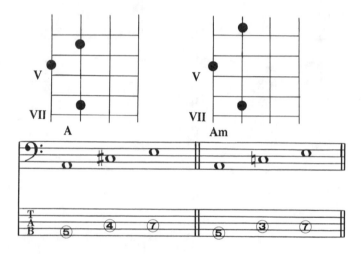

You can see that they each contain the root and the fifth of the A major scale. The note in between is the **third**. In the major chord it is a **major third** (from the major scale); in the minor chord it is a **minor third** (the major third flatted).

You can use these chord patterns to create riffs and lines like these:

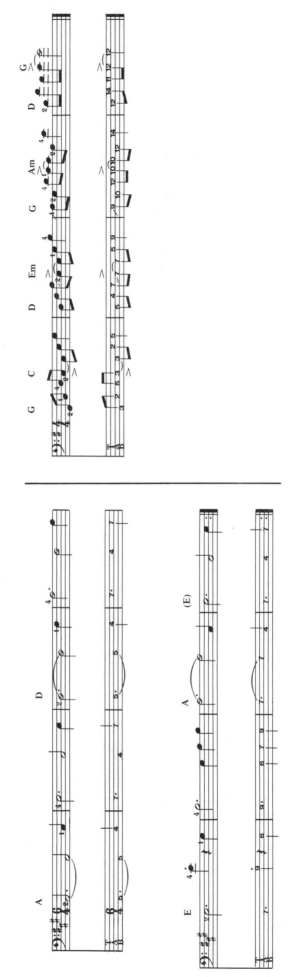

Here are two more riffs using other major and minor chord patterns. The first is in $\frac{6}{8}$, which is felt in two not unlike $\frac{6}{4}$. Here each beat consists of three eighth-notes and the backbeat accent on **four** is usually not as strong as in $\frac{6}{4}$. The typical $\frac{6}{8}$ rhythm is referred to as a **shuffle** rhythm.

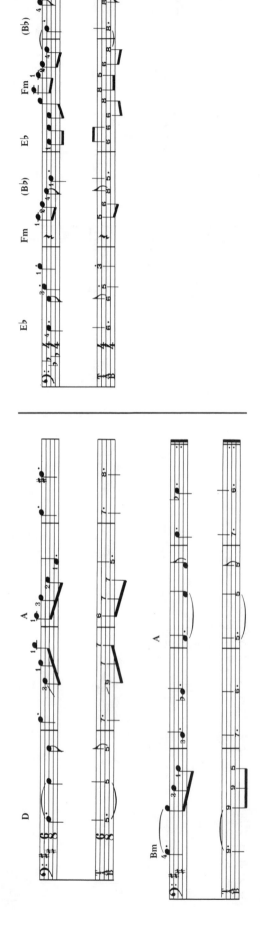

Sixth and Seventh Chords

Adding a **sixth** to the simple three-note chord pattern gives us familiar bass lines like these:

The first of these patterns is a standard **walking bass**. Adding a **seventh** to this pattern makes it more interesting.

If you play the major-scale pattern and count up to seven, you will find that the note that we have just added is different from the seventh note of the scale.

The seventh in a seventh chord is flatted compared to the seventh in the major scale of the same root. This is because the seventh in a seventh chord (like A7, E♭7, etc.) is derived from the seventh note above the V. This is why you will sometimes hear it referred to as a **dominant seventh** chord (another name for the V chord is the 'dominant').

It is not necessary to understand theoretically why this is so; what is important is to understand these moveable chord patterns and to be able to apply them.

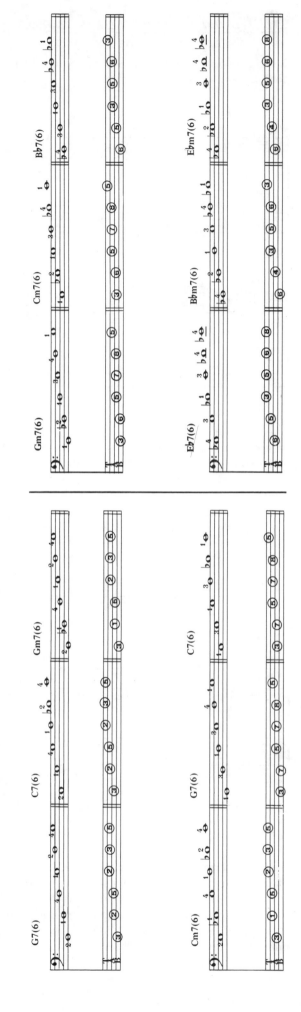

To finish off this chapter let's play a few more lines using sixth and seventh chords plus scale steps and chromatic passing tones. Notice which pattern or patterns each phrase is working out of. Also listen to how the in-clusion—or exclusion—of thirds, sixths, and sevenths affects the tonal color of each example.

* Two notes of different pitch joined by a curved line (looks just like a tie) indicates a **hammeron** or **pulloff**. In this case you play the open E string, then bring down your left-hand first finger on the first fret to sound the F. You can also hammer on from one fretted note to another. A pulloff is the opposite, whereby you sound a fretted note and "pull off" with the fretting finger to sound the open string or a lower fretted note. Watch for hammerons and pulloffs in the examples that follow.

42

Pentatonic Scales

A **pentatonic** scale is made up of five notes. There are hundreds of pentatonic scales possible, but only two are commonly used. The first is conveniently outlined by one of the most famous bass lines of all time: the opening bars of Smokey Robinson's "My Girl."

Comparing this with the major scale shows it to be made up of the first, second, third, fifth, and sixth degrees:

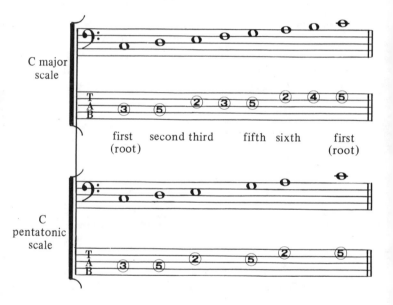

Another way to think of this major pentatonic scale is as a major sixth chord with one extra note, the second. Because of this there is not a whole lot new to say about using the major pentatonic scale to create lines. However, it can be very useful for creating fills.

As long as they sound good and make sense melodically, pentatonic fills will not clash with I, IV, or V chords. In fact, pentatonic lines like the ones above may be played against a variety of different progressions. Here is another fill which fits several alternate chord progressions.

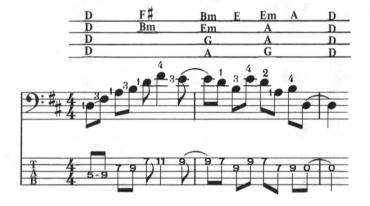

Now let's look at this pentatonic scale from a different slant. If we start on the fifth note of this scale, considering it the root of a new scale, we get a minor pentatonic scale:

This is often called a 'blues' scale because, again comparing it with a major scale, it has a flatted third and flatted seventh, which are characteristic blue notes.

Elvis Costello and Bruce Thomas

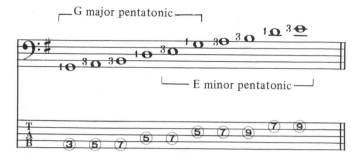

This blues scale is very useful as a point of departure for creating bass parts for blues, rock, or any other kind of pop music.

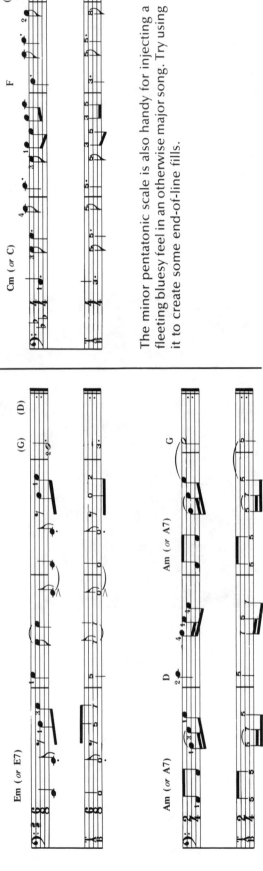

The minor pentatonic scale is also handy for injecting a fleeting bluesy feel in an otherwise major song. Try using it to create some end-of-line fills.

To sum it up, here are some common movable positions for major pentatonic scales. Study the fretboard diagrams to discover and learn the three basic patterns on which all of these scales are based.

Major Pentatonic Scales

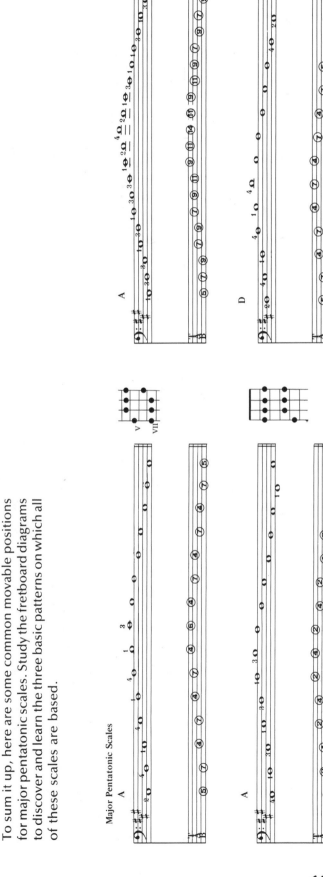

Minor Pentatonic (Blues) Scales

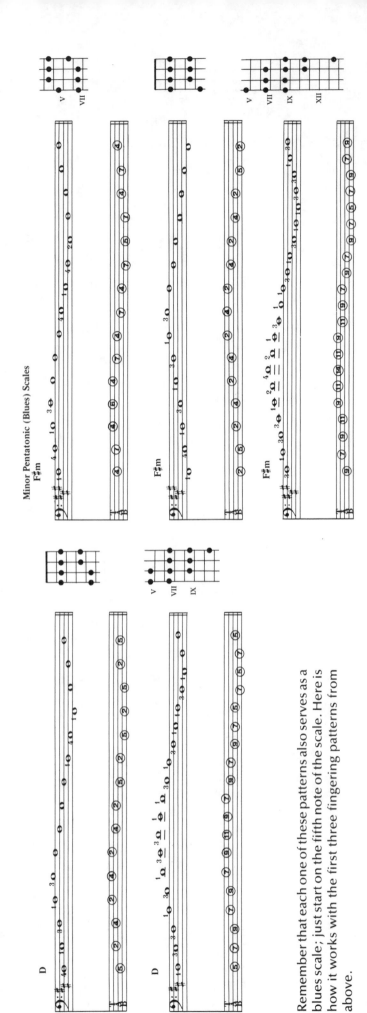

Remember that each one of these patterns also serves as a blues scale; just start on the fifth note of the scale. Here is how it works with the first three fingering patterns from above.

Styles

The information in this chapter is presented as a series of generalizations and tips to point you in the right direction. Obviously we cannot cover every aspect of stylistic nuance peculiar to every type of music. However, I believe you will find enough here to get you thinking along the right lines.

I would urge you to examine each of the sections carefully even if some of the styles—broad categories though they are—hold little or no interest for you. In a sense any type of music is derivative of other styles. This is especially evident in today's music scene where the edges of many genres are blurring or being stretched considerably through fusion and crossover—there are country bands playing rock and reggae, rock bands covering jazz standards, and so on. So even if your main interest is new wave music, you never know when you may be called on to come up with a convincing funk or rockabilly bass-line.

Country

Most country music is comparatively simple rhythmically, melodically, and harmonically. This seeming simplicity can actually make this music harder to play than some more complex types. For one thing, a lot of the success of the performance lies in your inherent emotion and a knowledgeable and sympathetic interpretation. For another, the sparse and uncluttered texture creates a transparency that makes the rhythm section's contribution much more vital—and its shortcomings much more obvious—than in denser, more complex musics.

Country bass-lines most often fall into the simple root/fifth category. Country bass-players usually lock in with the drummer's bass-drum pattern exactly. They also take great care to give each note its full value. A typical country touch comes from what I'll call **root doubling** (for lack of a better term). This is really a simple matter of making sure that the last note you play before a chord change is the root of the chord. In a root/fifth line this means that you either have to repeat the root or double back to it before going to the root of the next chord.

or

Nick Lowe

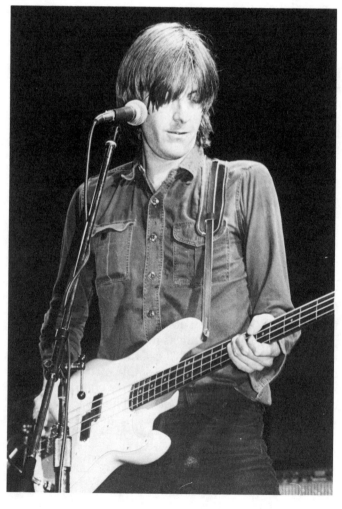

Here is a slightly longer example:

Another common country bass practice—especially in Western swing and honky tonk music—is the use of the simple walking bass:

Here is an example using a lot of country variations of
the standard walking bass line:

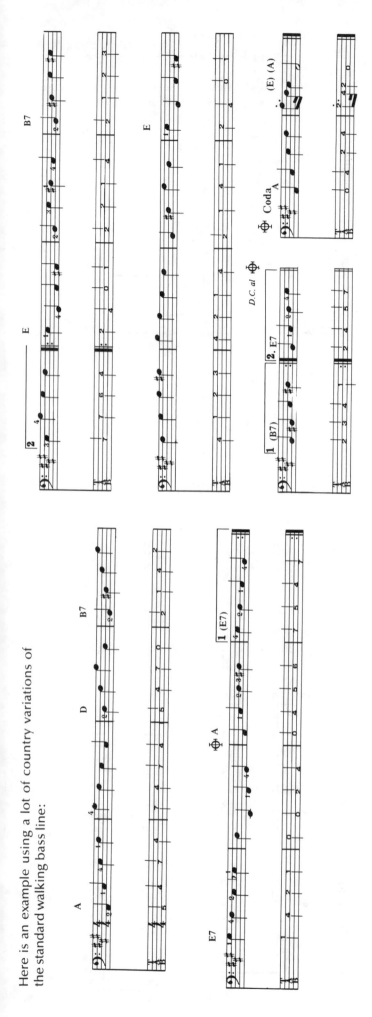

The basis of most blues rhythm is the shuffle. Most often, blues bass-lines are developed around the notes of the blues scale (minor pentatonic) and spend a lot of time on the roots of chords rather than alternating between root and fifth.

Here are a few sample patterns that could be developed into bass parts for standard blues songs:

Notice that these are written in $\frac{12}{8}$ time, which is like $\frac{6}{8}$ except that there are four groups of three to each measure instead of two.

Other common types of blues bass-lines are the walking bass in shuffle rhythm,

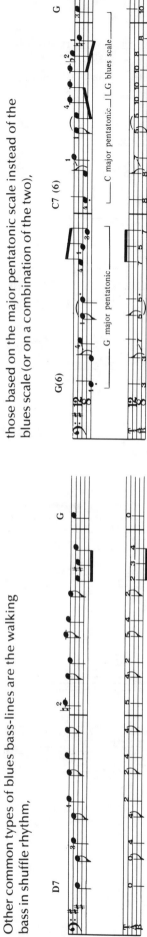

or this distinctly bluesy variation,

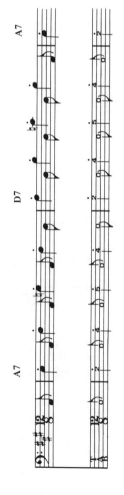

those based on the major pentatonic scale instead of the blues scale (or on a combination of the two),

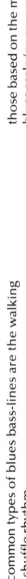

54

and for those slow blues with a backbeat (best thought of in $\frac{6}{4}$ with an accent on the **four** of each measure and a lesser accent on **one**).

It is a convention in blues tunes that each verse ends with two measures known as a **turnaround.** The turnaround causes the chord progression to end on the V chord, which then sends you back to the beginning. The turnaround could be a simple I IV I V^7,

or the standard I I^7 IV $\flat VI^7$ V^7 $\flat VI^7$ V^{7*} or I I^7 IV IVm I V^7

---

*   For the theoretically minded among you, the $\flat VI^7$ chord in this turnaround is actually a $II^7\flat5$, which is the V of the V chord.

** In **slash chords**, the second half of the chord name indicates which note other than the root of the chord should be played in the bass.

or this jazzy I VI^7 II^7 V^7.

Rock

Since rock originally was born of blues and country, a lot of the ideas we have just covered apply to this section as well. In older rock and roll tunes from the fifties and sixties you will find ample opportunity to use walking bass patterns, shuffle rhythm, and turnarounds. In rock ballads you will often be playing with a backbeat feel and/or developing your lines from the major pentatonic scale.

Most contemporary rock music is such a mixed bag that it is difficult to make too many generalizations. Luckily, most bands are made up of four or five musicians at most and the bass is usually prominent enough in the mix so that you can hear and study the lines. Anyway, here are a few observations on rock bass-lines.

In rock, more so than in other types of music, the bass often participates in playing **hooks**. A hook is any melodic figure (usually rhythmically interesting as well) that is repeated at specific points in the song, or throughout certain sections of the song, and which forms part of the song's identity. Most of the time the hook is played in octaves by bass and guitar. To give you the idea, here are four of the most famous bass/guitar hooks of all time:

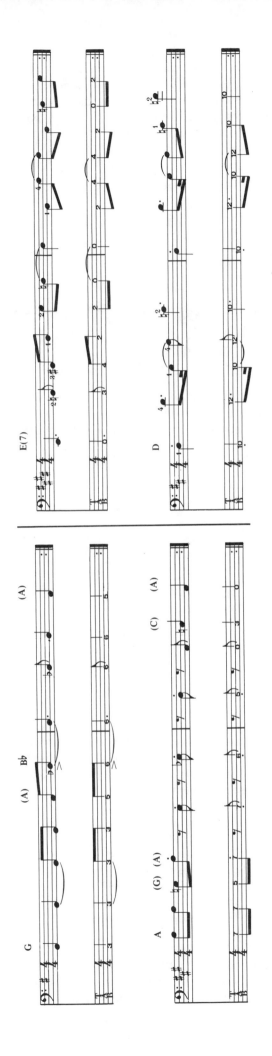

A lot of bass players, especially those who play rock, use picks. It is pretty easy to get the hang of and makes certain moves a lot easier. Most players use a heavy or medium guitar pick of the standard teardrop shape. There are also picks of different shapes and sizes, and some of the larger ones may be easier to get a grip on at first.

Whatever shape you decide on—and picks are conveniently cheap enough for you to experiment with several varieties—you hold it like this:

Your hand should be as relaxed as possible so that the pick rests on your curled index finger while the thumb holds it in place. The idea is to allow the pick to be as flexible as possible without your dropping it.

One of the advantages of playing with a pick is that it makes playing a fast string of consecutive notes easy when you use alternating **downstrokes** and **upstrokes**. The movement should come mostly from the wrist but you can put some force behind each stroke by using your forearm a bit also. A downstroke (⊓) is down toward the floor and an upstroke (Ⅴ) is up toward the ceiling.

Try these rock bass-lines following the picking indications carefully. Make sure that your alternative picking sounds even (except where accents are indicated). Avoid the tendency to play harder on the downstrokes.

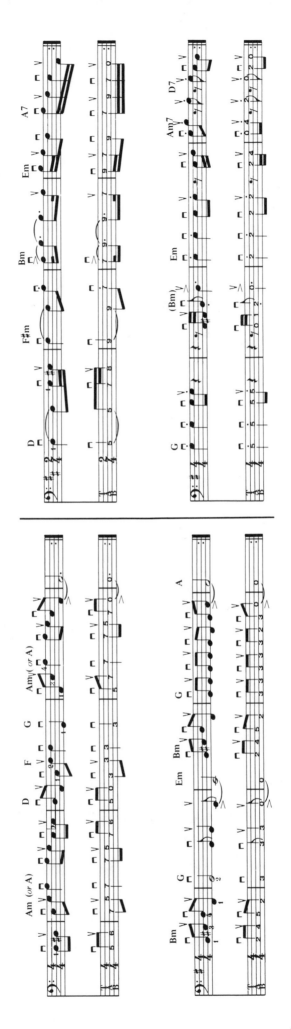

Playing with a pick calls for a new technique of right-hand damping. It is done with the heel of the hand fairly close to the bridge like this:

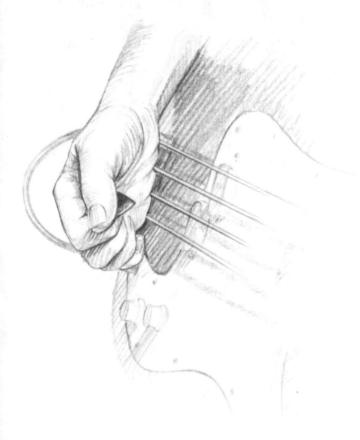

If you rest your hand very close to the bridge, you will discover that you can play and the strings will not be completely damped but only **muted**. This is a good, funky effect when used sparingly. Try these next riffs muting each note marked with a cross (+). Even if they are muted, be sure to hold out each note for its proper time-value.

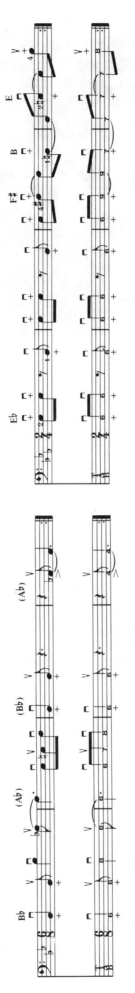

One more tip on playing rock bass: Keep in mind the root/fifth/octave positions introduced way back at the beginning of this book.

Leland Sklar

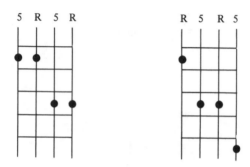

Since most rock tunes use simple **triads** (three-note chords like the ones we discussed in the chapter, "Chords") to harmonize the melody, you should keep the bass part harmonically simple as well. Often the rhythm guitar will be playing only open fifths as opposed to complete chords. If the bass part includes a lot of thirds, sixths, and sevenths, it detracts from the effect of raw, stark power. One brief example: While the first of these two parts sounds okay, the second interpretation is definitely the correct one for most rock idioms.

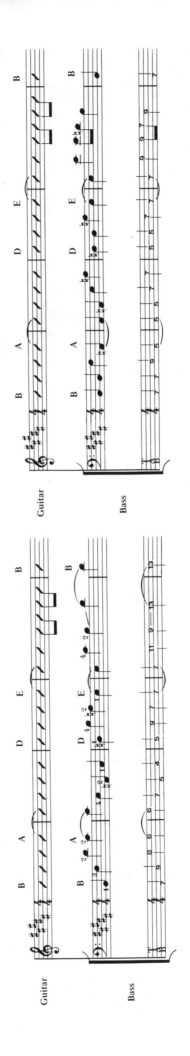

Here are a few more riffs and lines based on and around those root/fifth positions.

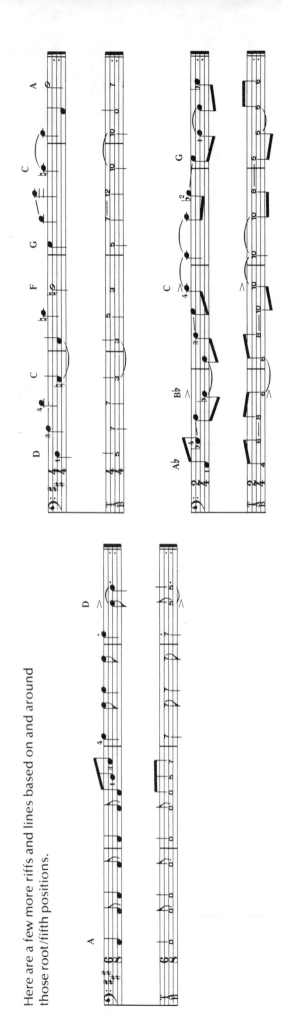

Since the main idea of some of the more avant-garde new music is the flouting of conventional rules, it is pointless to try to lay down any law. However, many new-wave bass parts are similar to simple rock lines, so we will take a look at a couple of typical examples. Play these lines with a pick and notice how the use of repeated downstrokes can create a driving—or even frantic, if desired—kind of pulse.

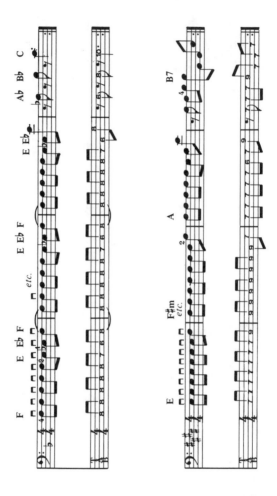

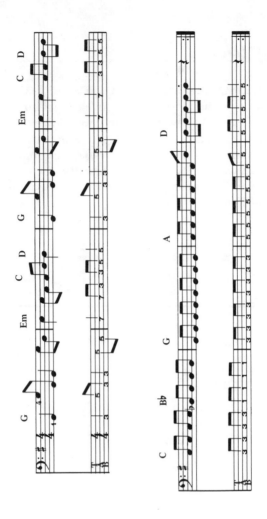

Rockabilly

Although rockabilly was first played by country musicians imitating blues and jazz, what it quickly became was rock and roll. To get a good handle on rockabilly, try listening to early rock and roll recordings by Bill Haley, Jerry Lee Lewis, or Elvis Presley.

All authentic rockabilly bass players in the early fifties played standup bass. One of the characteristic effects they used was 'slapping' the strings, which added a particular percussive drive to simple root/fifth lines. This technique is unfortunately not possible on electric bass.

When they weren't slapping the bass, those early rockers made extensive use of walking bass variations like these:

𝒢𝓊𝓃𝓀

Funk bass-lines are without a doubt the most demanding. Even in tunes with a fairly simple groove, the bass part can be highly complex—usually more so than the guitar or keyboard parts. Add to this the difficult techniques of **string popping** and **thumb slaps** and you end up with a job for Superman.

Let's start out by taking a look at the two special techniques mentioned above. String popping, or **snapping**, is usually employed on one of the two top strings to produce a percussive, staccato attack. To pop a string, you hook your right-hand index finger under it, pull it straight out from the fingerboard, and let it snap back. The note is usually damped immediately by releasing the pressure of the left-hand fretting finger. Try this riff, popping the notes marked **P**.

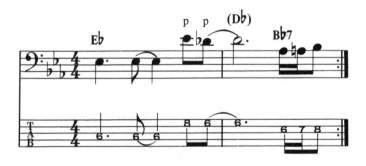

String pops are often combined with hammerons and pulloffs.

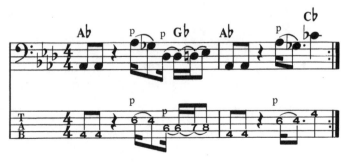

Thumb slaps are usually executed on the two bottom strings. To slap a string, form your right hand into a loose fist with the thumb sticking out parallel to the string.

Keeping your thumb straight but loose, bring it down sharply on the string with a twisting motion of the forearm. The note is sounded by the string slapping against the upper frets. You will have to experiment to find just the right spot on your bass but it should be somewhere on or just beyond the end of the neck.

If you are doing it right, your thumb should feel like it is bouncing back from the string. This bounce makes it easy to play two notes in a row with the first being accented, giving the effect of an echo. Try the last riff with thumb slaps (S) on the low notes.

The combination of thumb slaps and string pops makes it natural to create highly syncopated rhythms. One common syncopation is produced by the following octave riff.

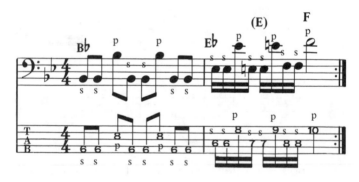

The Blues Brothers: Steve Cropper, Dan Akroyd, Duck Dunn, John Belushi, and Matt "Guitar" Murphy

Along the same lines, you can slap a string that is completely damped to add a purely percussive accent to this kind of syncopation. The damping is accomplished primarily by the left hand but it may be necessary to bring the heel of your right hand down on the strings as well. What you should hear is the characteristic "click" of the regular thumb slap but accompanied by a low "thud" from the muffled string. This type of **slap damping** is indicated by an **X** instead of a note head or fret number.

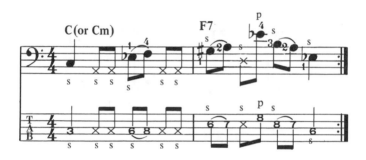

Developing this idea a little further produces these types of sophisticated syncopations. Practice each of these riffs slowly at first and observe the accent patterns carefully. Some of them may not make too much sense until you speed them up, but you will have trouble playing them up to tempo until you have mastered the coordination required by the various sequences of hand movements.

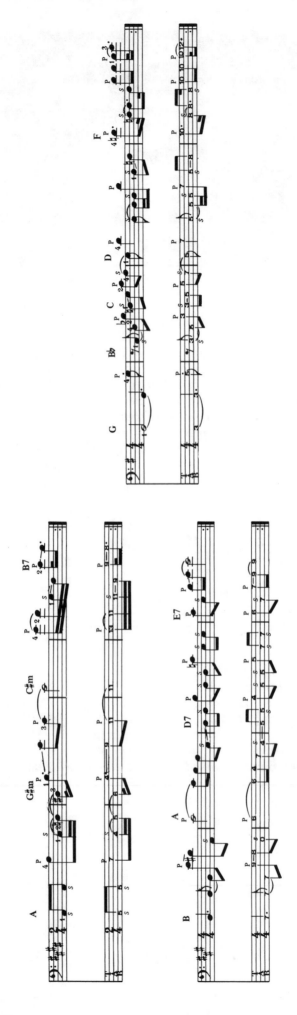

Although we talked about chords in a previous chapter, I have waited until now to discuss playing more than one note simultaneously. Playing two notes at once is called a **double stop**. Try plucking these double stops on the top two strings with your index and middle fingers using a motion halfway between a rest stroke and a string pop.

Here are a few ways to work double stops into funk bass-lines. Notice that the most common double stops are thirds on the first and second strings,

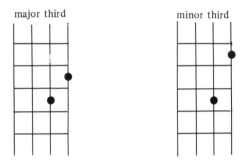

tenths on the first and fourth strings,

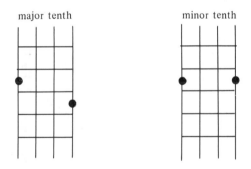

and **tritones** (flatted fifths) on the first and second strings.

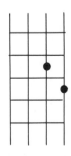

---

* The symbol ✕ is a **double sharp**. It raises the pitch of the note it precedes by a whole step (two half-steps). You may also see a **double flat** (♭♭) from time to time.

72

Steve Swallow

Jazz

In its way, jazz is probably as vague a term as is rock. One thing that can be said for all jazz tunes, however, is that their chord progressions are often quite complex, with changes coming two or more to the measure. This is a real problem on fast tunes when you want to play a walking bass-line. One thing that can save you is to learn to recognize the ubiquitous II V I progression.

The II V I progression shows up in every kind of music but in jazz it seems to have been elevated to a kind of religion. The trick to playing a walking line through a set of changes like this is to be aware of them ahead of time so that you can make up your line from the major scale of the I chord. For instance, here is a fragment of a typical jazz tune:

Notice how the bass line follows the temporary changes of key implied by each II V I sequence:

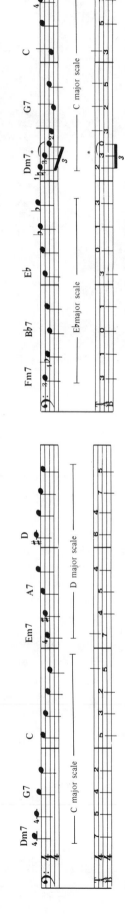

The II V I progression works because the II is the V of the V chord and so has the same strong pull toward V that V has toward I. Taking this one step farther, we can add the V of the II chord, the VI, in front to get a VI II V I progression.

---

* A group of three eight-notes with a 3 on the beam is a **triplet**. Play the three notes evenly in the space of one quarter-note.

Here is the chord progression to part of a well-known jazz standard with all of the II V I and VI II V I progressions, and the scales they imply, identified.

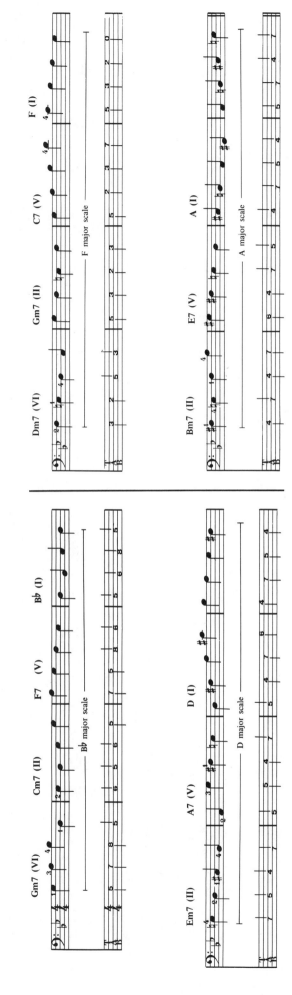

75

A common device in playing II V I progressions is to flat the fifth of some of the chords. Since the fifth of the V chord is always one whole-step above the root of the I, flatting the fifth so that it is only a half-step away makes for a very smooth transition from V to I. The same holds true for II to V and for VI to II. Here are the first few bars of the last example using flatted fifths.

A large portion of the jazz repertoire mimics traditional South American rhythms such as the **samba** and the **mambo.** These are a lot of fun to play, not least of all because the **pocket,** or groove, is easily established by fitting a simple root/fifth line into the regular rhythmic pattern. Try these examples to get the idea.

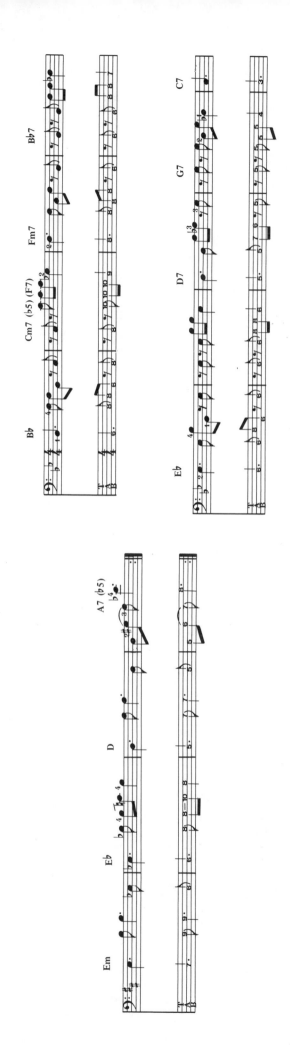

Bibliography

Here are a few books that I have found useful at various times. Each one has a slightly different slant but all are excellent texts for the bass player wanting more than this small overview can offer.

Anderton, Craig. **Guitar Gadgets.** New York: Amsco Publications, 1983.
> Don't let the title fool you; if you want information on effects boxes, this is the book. All of the information is easily translatable from guitar to bass language and there are even a few specific hints for applying certain effects to bass.

Berle, Arnie. **How to Play Bass Guitar.** New York: Acorn Music Press, 1981.
> Although intended for use with a teacher, you may get something out of this one on your own. It gets very repetitive but you get a lot of practice reading root/fifth, scale, and chord based lines in every key. (Standard notation with instruction in note reading.)

Gross, David. **Teach Yourself Rock Bass.** New York: Amsco Music Publishing Company, 1978.
> This is a fairly basic book but will give you extensive practice in typical rock rhythms and chord progressions. (Standard notation and tablature.)

Laird, Rick. **Improvising Jazz Bass.** New York: Consolidated Music Publishers, 1980.
> A comprehensive survey of modern jazz-bass technique, this one gets somewhat thorny. It offers practice in odd time-signatures, modal playing, chord scales, and has a fantastic section on usual and unusual pentatonic scales. (Standard notation only.)

Laird, Rick. **Jazz Riffs for Bass.** New York: Amsco Music Publishing Company, 1978.
> A scaled-down version of the above. **Recommended.** (Standard notation only.)

Novick, Adam. **Harmonics for Electric Bass.** Eugene, Oregon: Free-Bass Press (distributed by Music Sales Corporation), 1980.
> If you are intrigued by the chime-like sound of harmonics, this book can help you explore ways to use them musically. (Standard notation with extensive fretboard diagrams.)

Starer, Robert. **Rhythmic Training for Musicians.** New York: MCA Music, 1969.
  If the notation of the rhythms in this book have given you trouble, here is a text which will give you a multitude of graded, progressive exercises in rhythm alone. **Recommended.**

Wolk, Tom. **Rock Riffs for Bass.** New York: Amsco Music Publishing Company, 1978.
  A compendium of riffs, fills, and longer lines grouped chronologically and stylistically to cover every style from fifties rock and roll to modern soul/funk and disco. **Recommended.** (Standard notation only.)

Wooten,Red. **Supplemental Studies for Electric Bass, String Bass, Tuba.** Hollywood: Try Publishing Company (distributed by Professional Drum Shop, Inc.), 1967.
  This funky little book has a wealth of information in it if you can figure out what Red is talking about. (He assumes a lot.) There is very little text and most of the music is pretty advanced, but if you stay with it you will learn a lot about reading from charts and playing in styles from gospel to **montuno** in every key known to man. **Recommended.**(Standard notation only.)